Hawthorn
001

Ivy and Forget-me-not
002

Daisy and Forget-me-not
003

Fuchsia and Heather
004

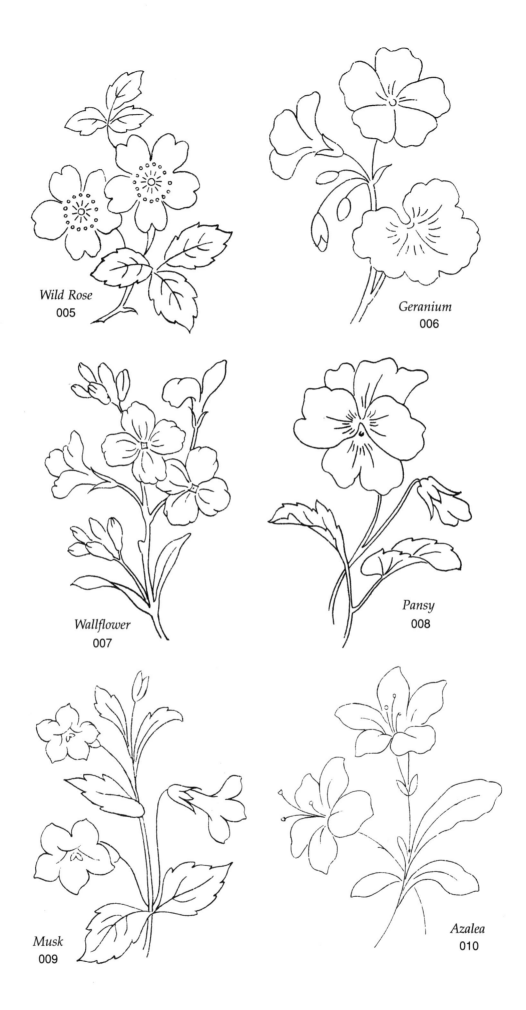

Wild Rose
005

Geranium
006

Wallflower
007

Pansy
008

Musk
009

Azalea
010

2

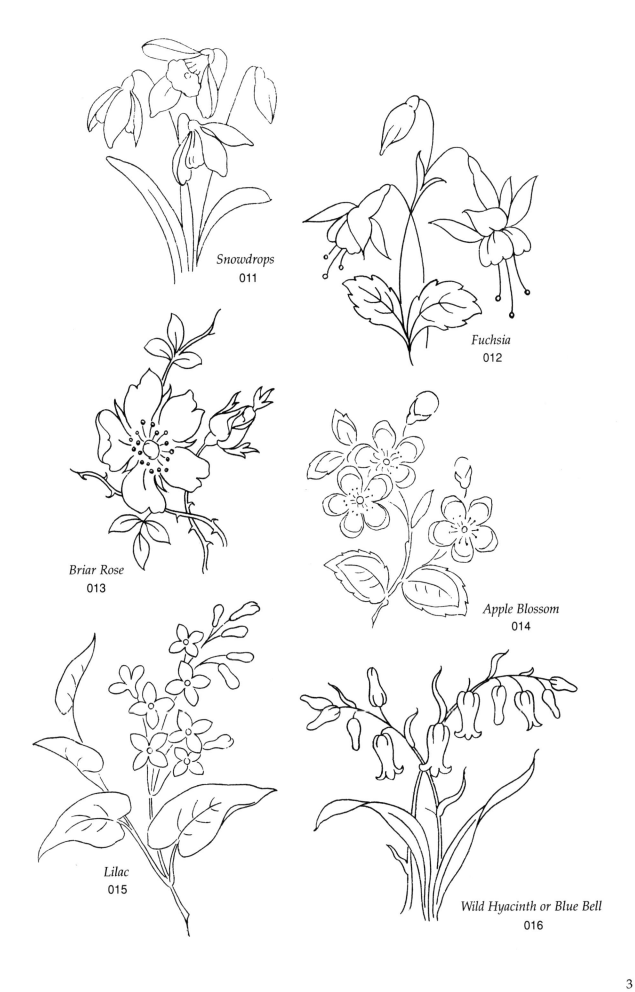

Snowdrops
011

Fuchsia
012

Briar Rose
013

Apple Blossom
014

Lilac
015

Wild Hyacinth or Blue Bell
016

3

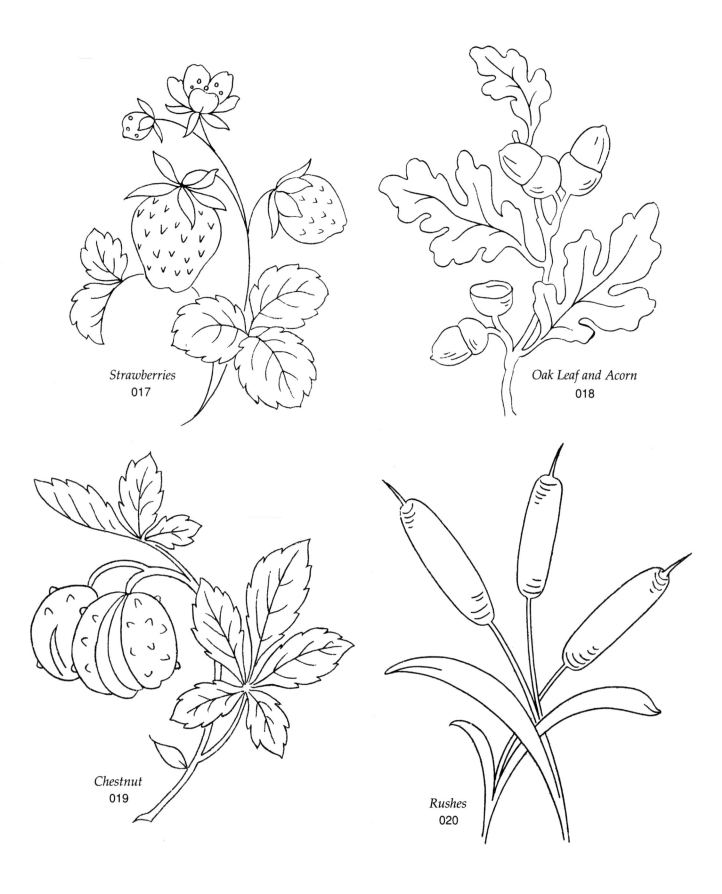

Strawberries
017

Oak Leaf and Acorn
018

Chestnut
019

Rushes
020

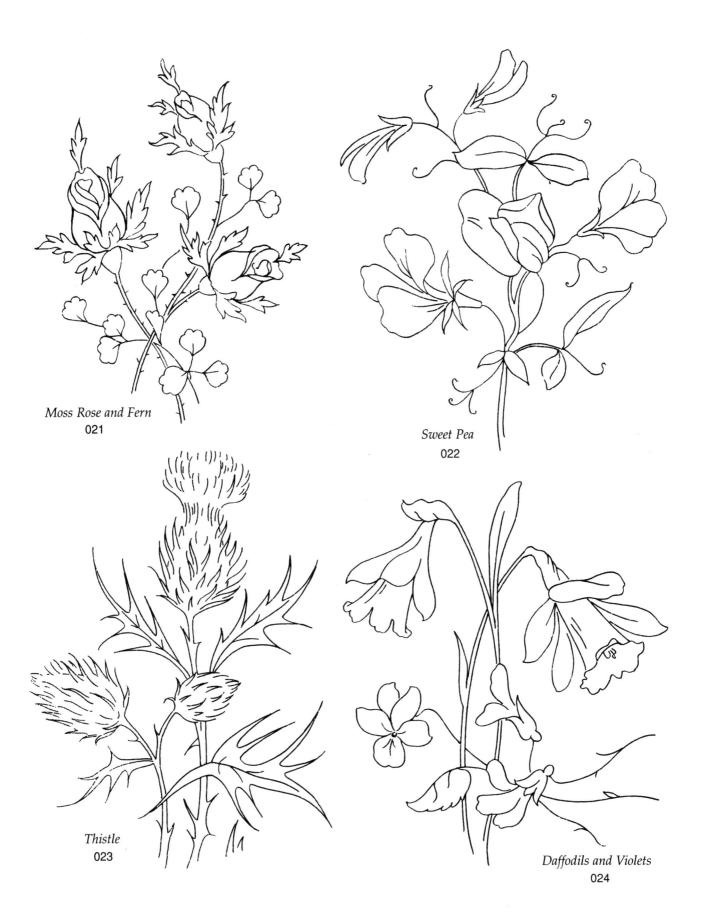

Moss Rose and Fern
021

Sweet Pea
022

Thistle
023

Daffodils and Violets
024

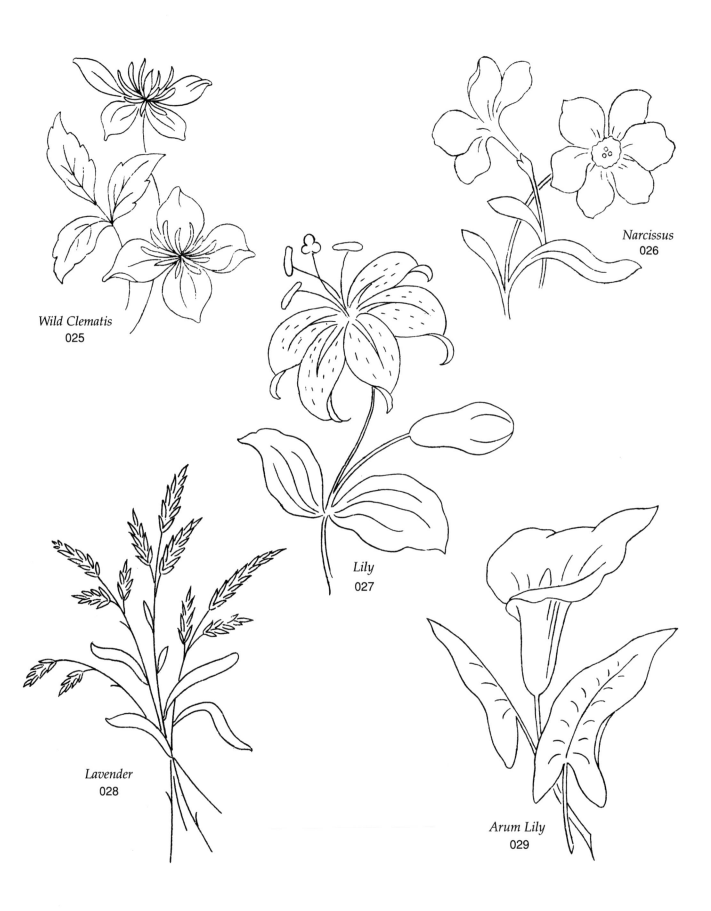

Wild Clematis
025

Narcissus
026

Lily
027

Lavender
028

Arum Lily
029

Rhododendron
030

Orchid
031

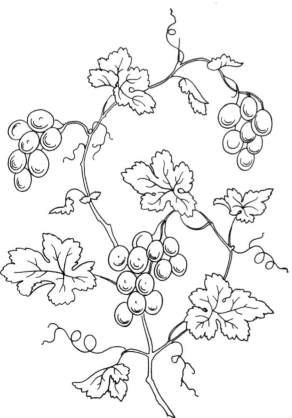

Vine
032

Convolvulus
033

7

Begonia
034

Chrysanthemum
035

Daisy
036

Poppy
037

Arum Lily
038

Thistle
039

Marigold
040

Chestnut
041

042

043

044

045

046

047

048

049

050

051

052

053

054

055

056

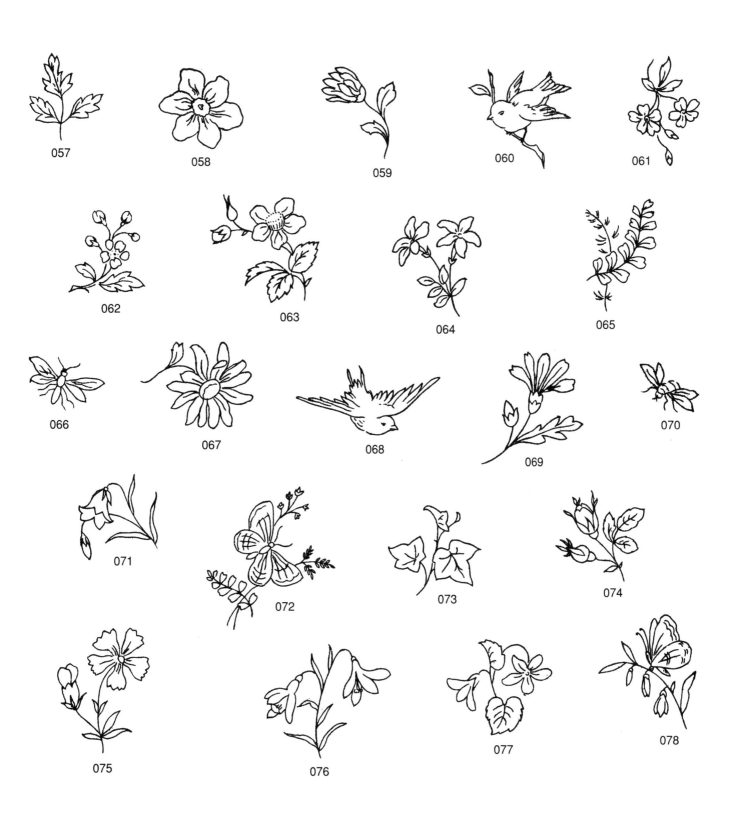

057

058

059

060

061

062

063

064

065

066

067

068

069

070

071

072

073

074

075

076

077

078

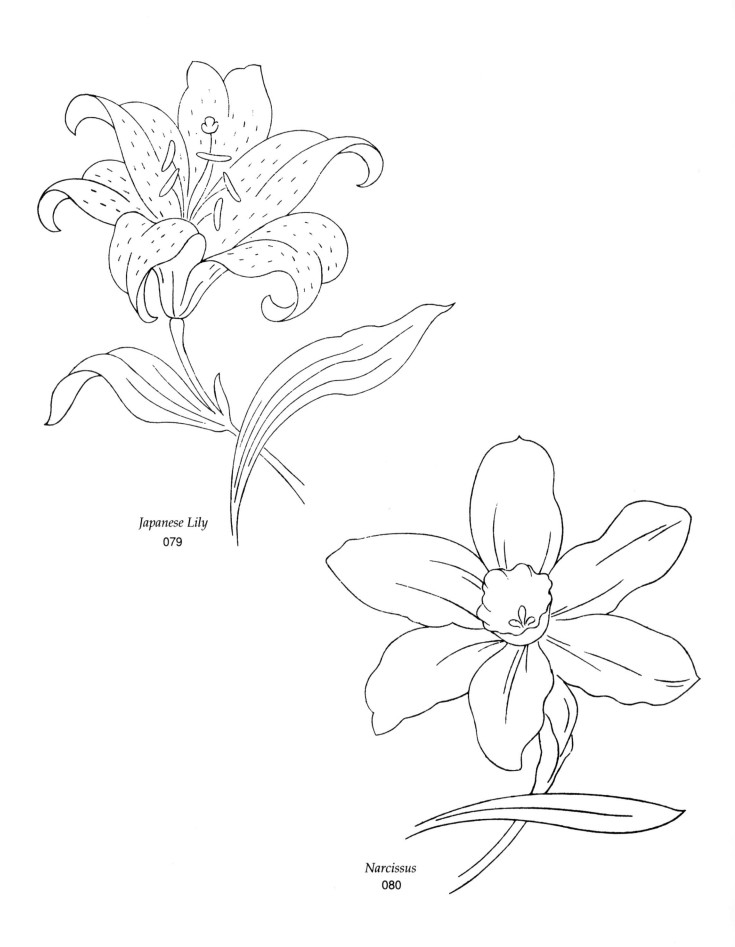

Japanese Lily
079

Narcissus
080

Poppy
081

Tulip
082

13

Pansy
083

Daffodil
084

085

086

Daisies

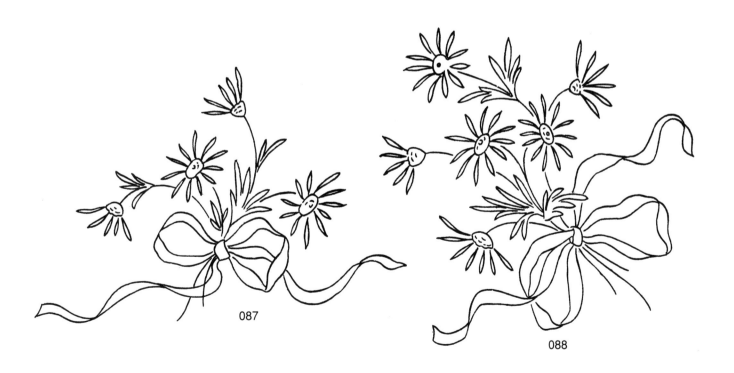

087

088

Flowering Rush
089

Daffodil
090

Lilac
091

Chrysanthemum
092

Wild Rose and Jessamine
093

Tiger Lily
094

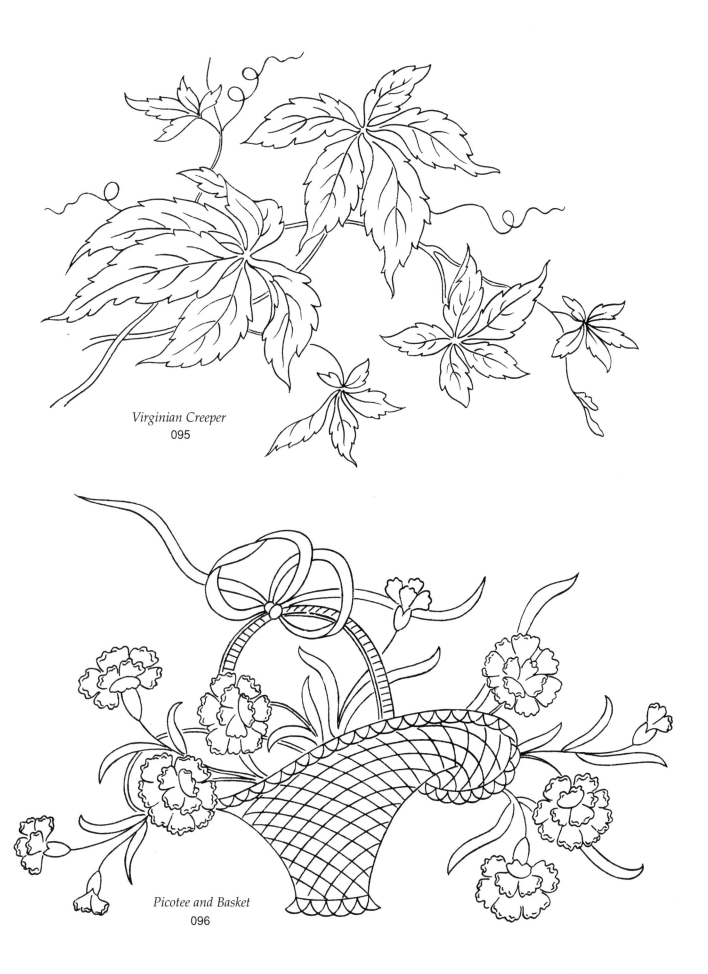

Virginian Creeper
095

Picotee and Basket
096

Wild Rose
097

Daisy
098

Poppy
099

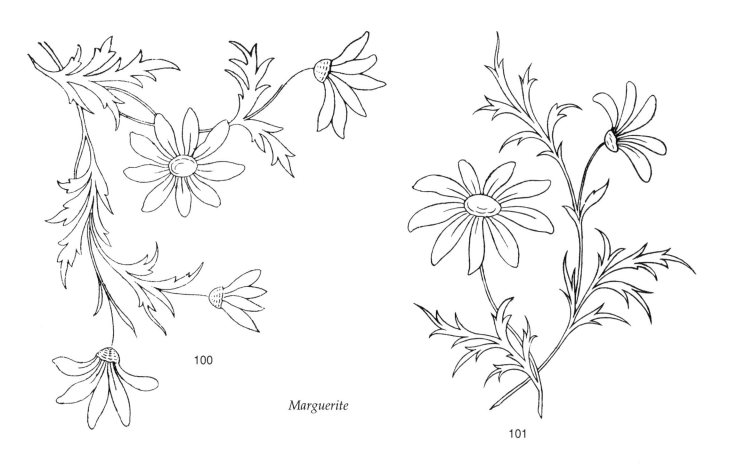

100

Marguerite

101

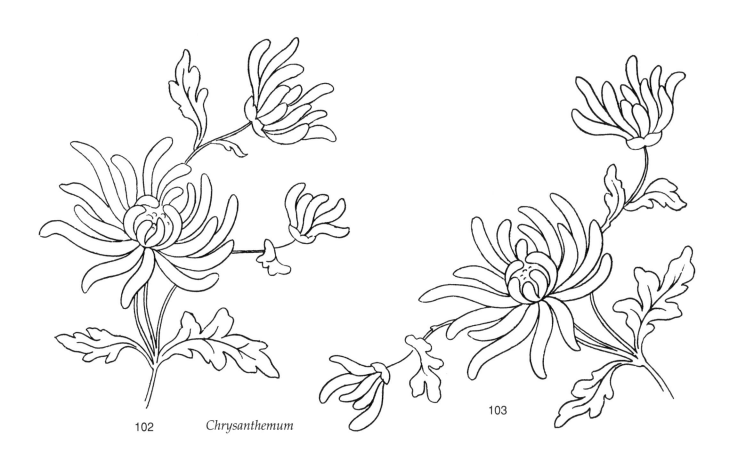

102   *Chrysanthemum*

103

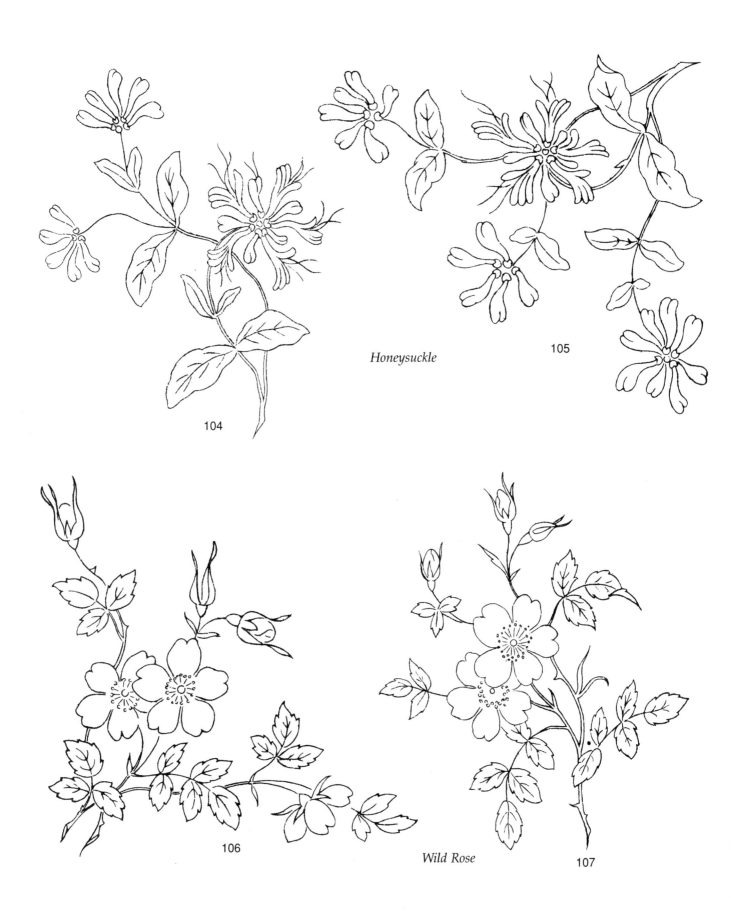

Honeysuckle

104

105

106

Wild Rose

107

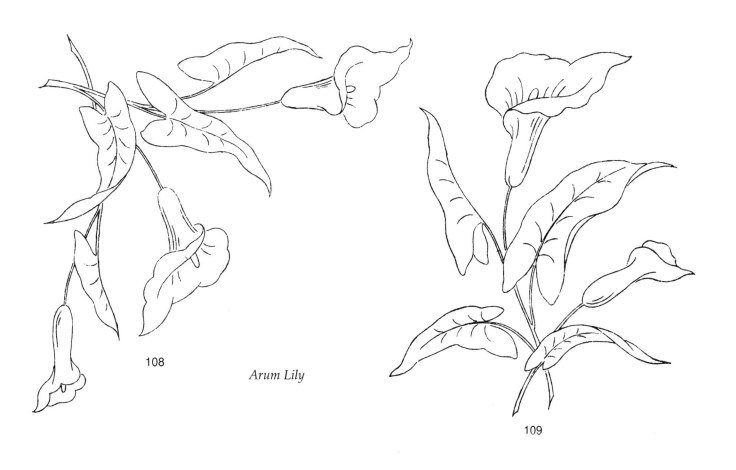

108

Arum Lily

109

110

Wild Rose and Jessamine

111

23

Azalea and Fern

112

113

114

Tiger Lily

115

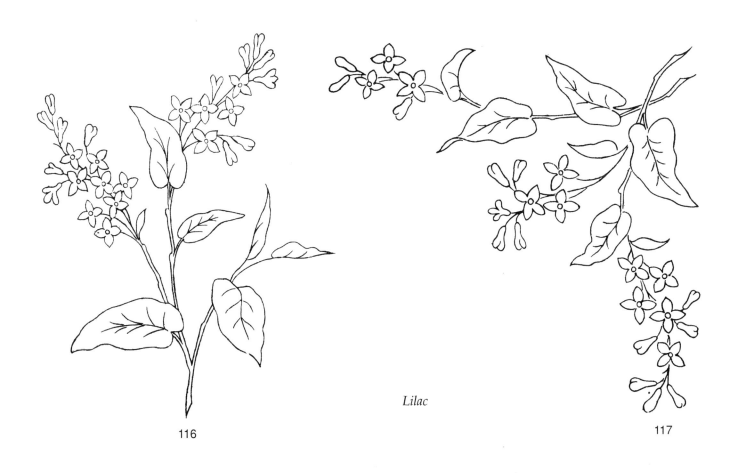

Lilac

116

117

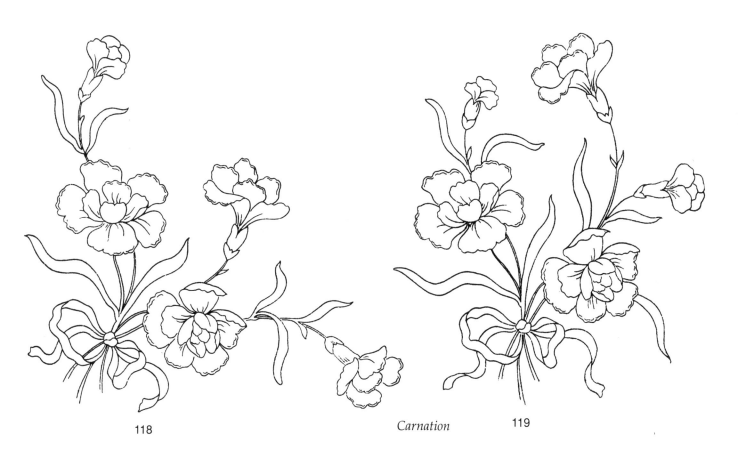

118

Carnation

119

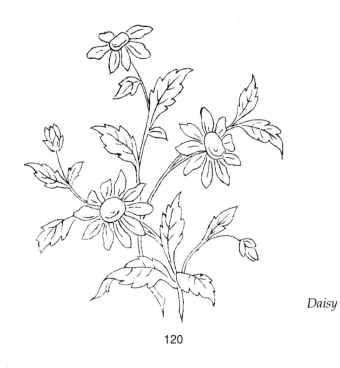

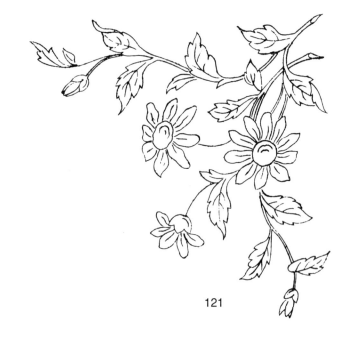

Daisy

120

121

122

123

Passion Flower

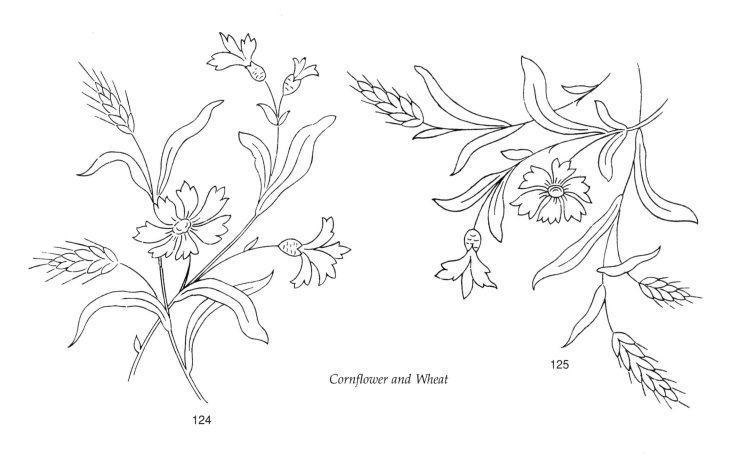

Cornflower and Wheat

125

124

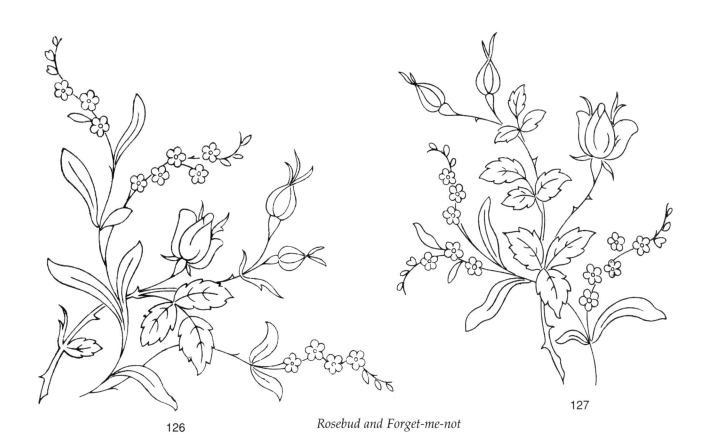

Rosebud and Forget-me-not

127

126

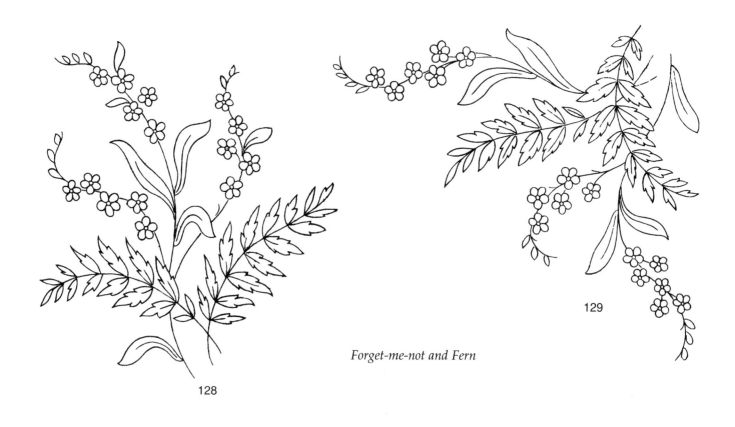

Forget-me-not and Fern

128

129

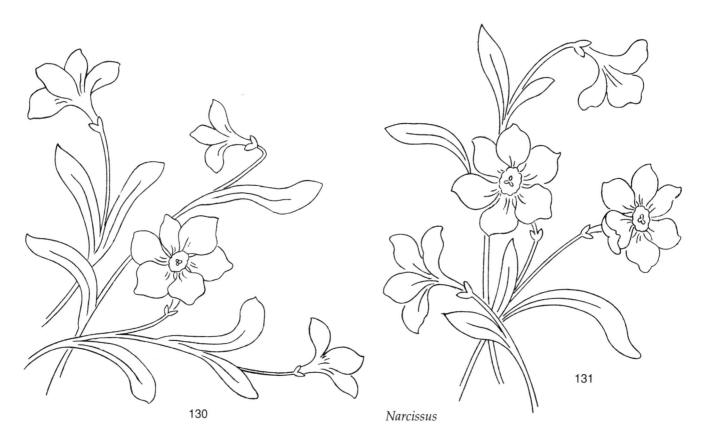

130

131

Narcissus

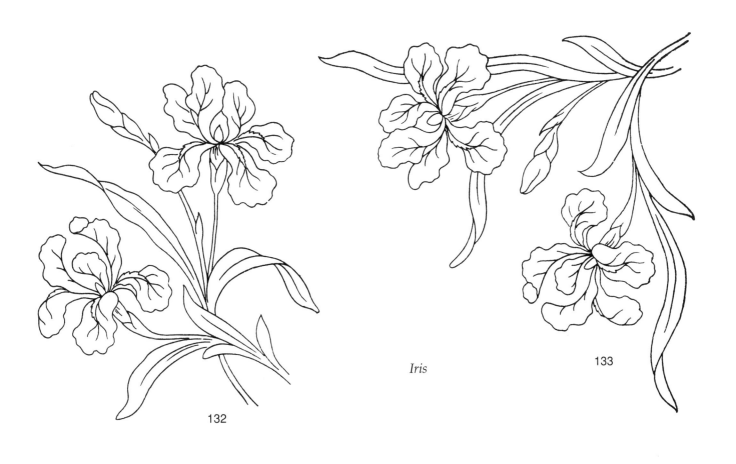

Iris

132

133

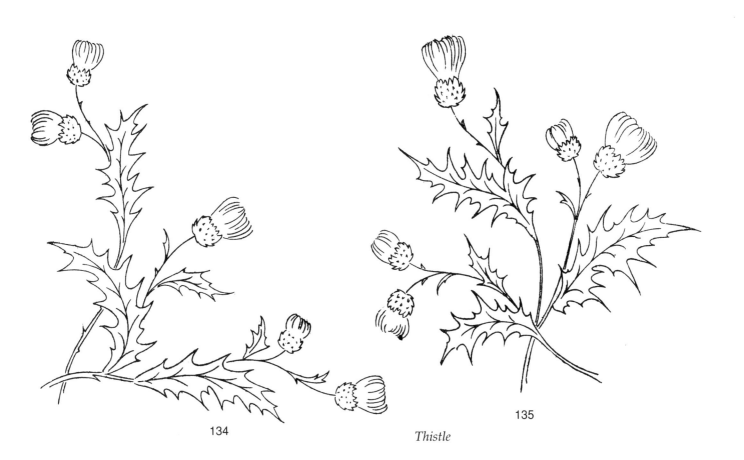

134

135

Thistle

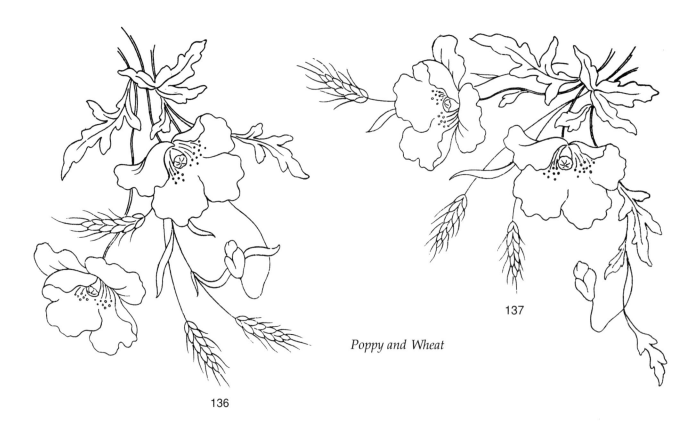

137

Poppy and Wheat

136

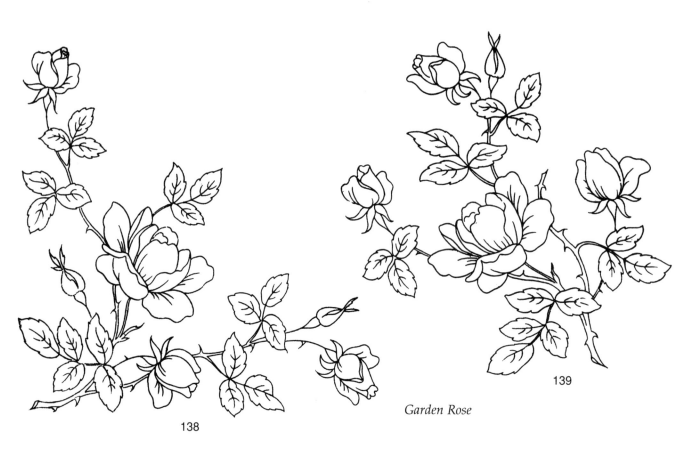

139

Garden Rose

138

30

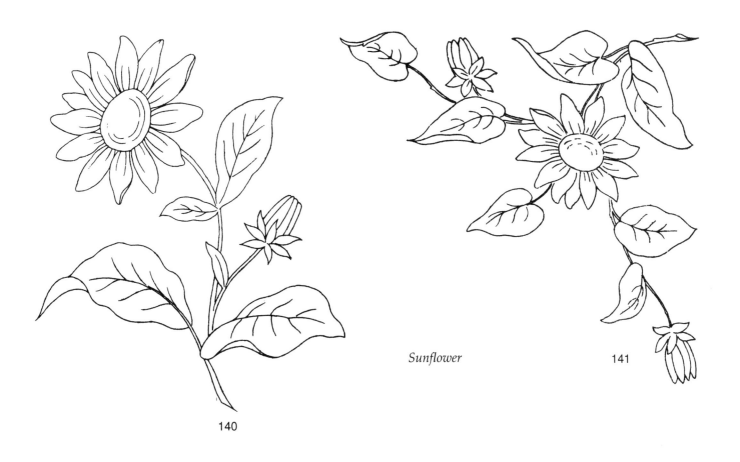

Sunflower

140

141

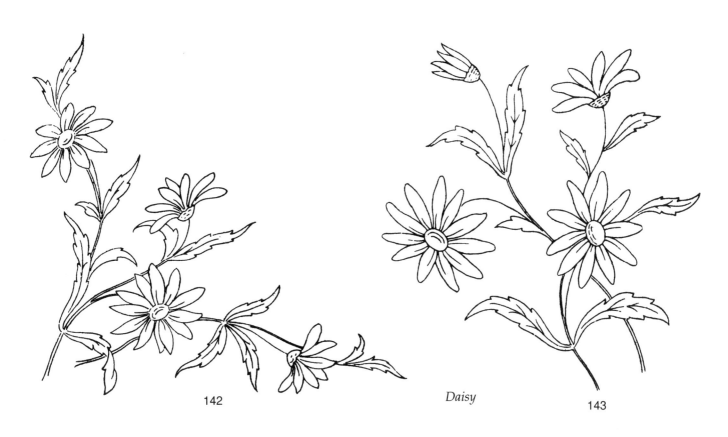

142

Daisy

143

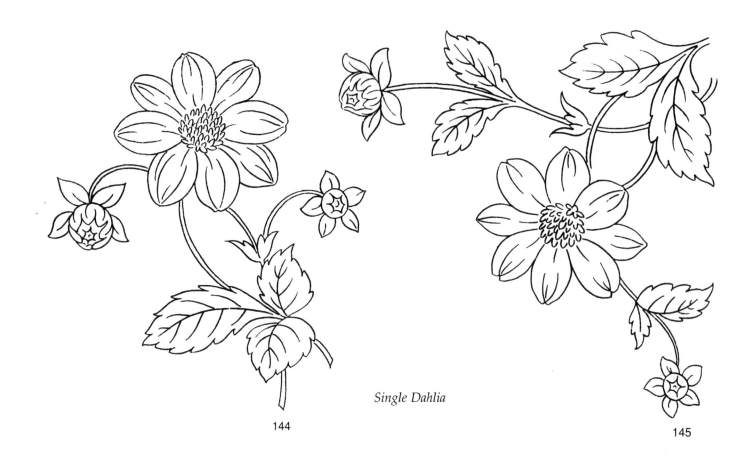

Single Dahlia

144

145

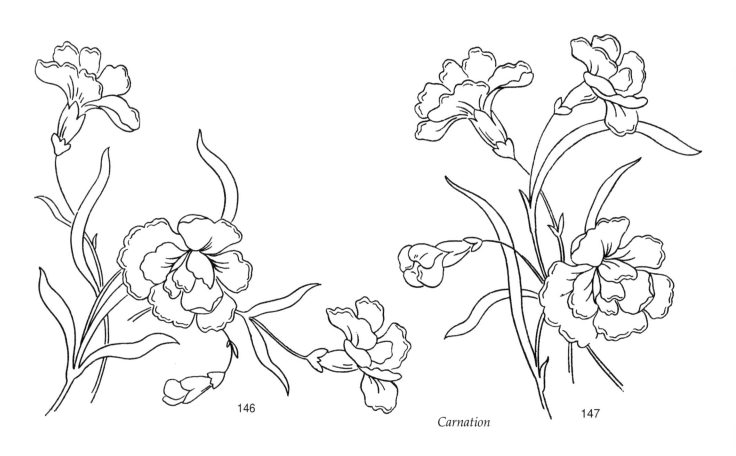

146

Carnation

147

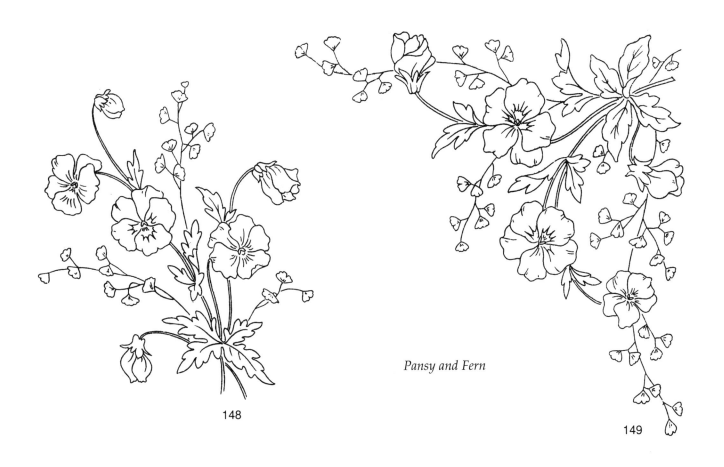

Pansy and Fern

148

149

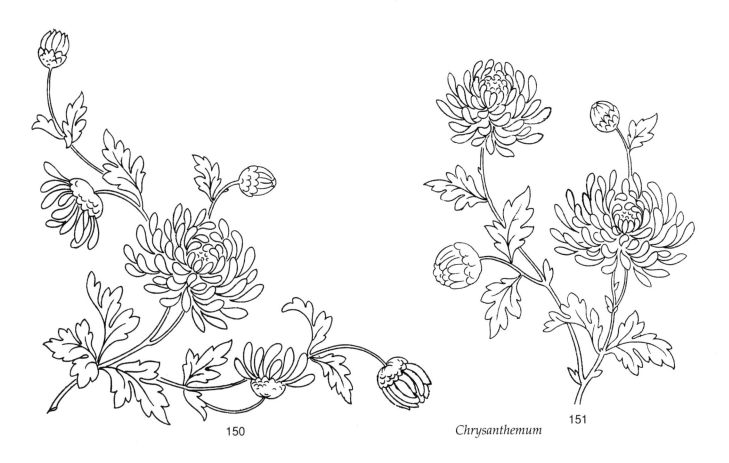

150

Chrysanthemum

151

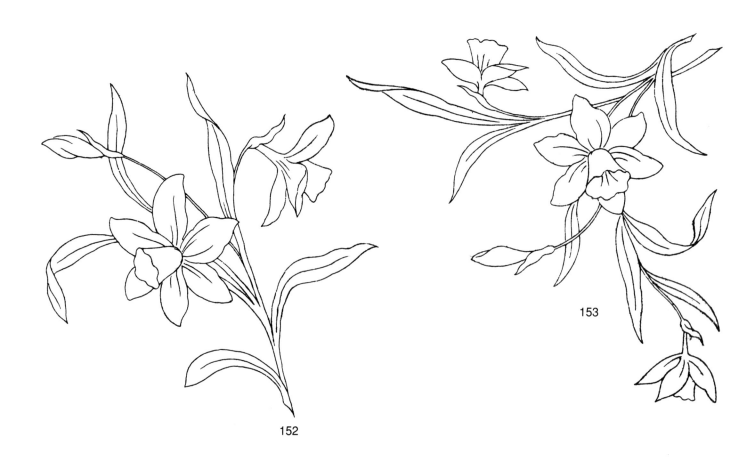

152

153

Daffodil

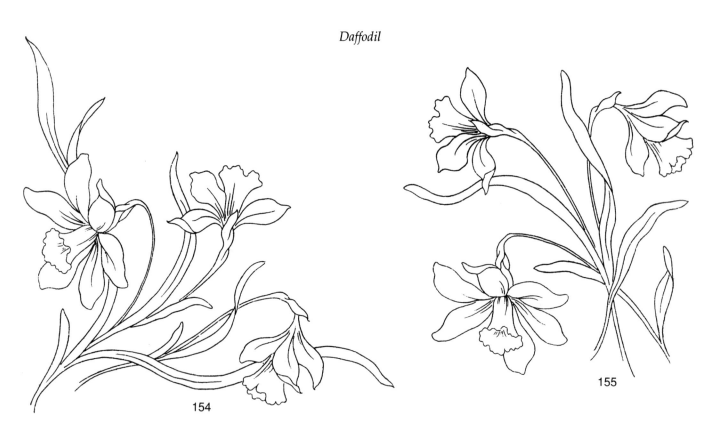

154

155

156

Tulip

157

158

Single Peony

159

160

Tiger Lily

161

162

Poppy   163

164

Gladiola

165

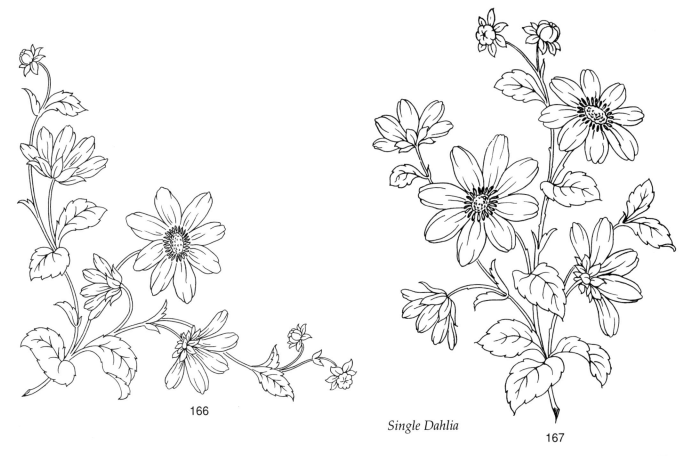

166

Single Dahlia

167

Marguerite
168

Cornflower
169

Carnations
170

Cabbage Roses
171

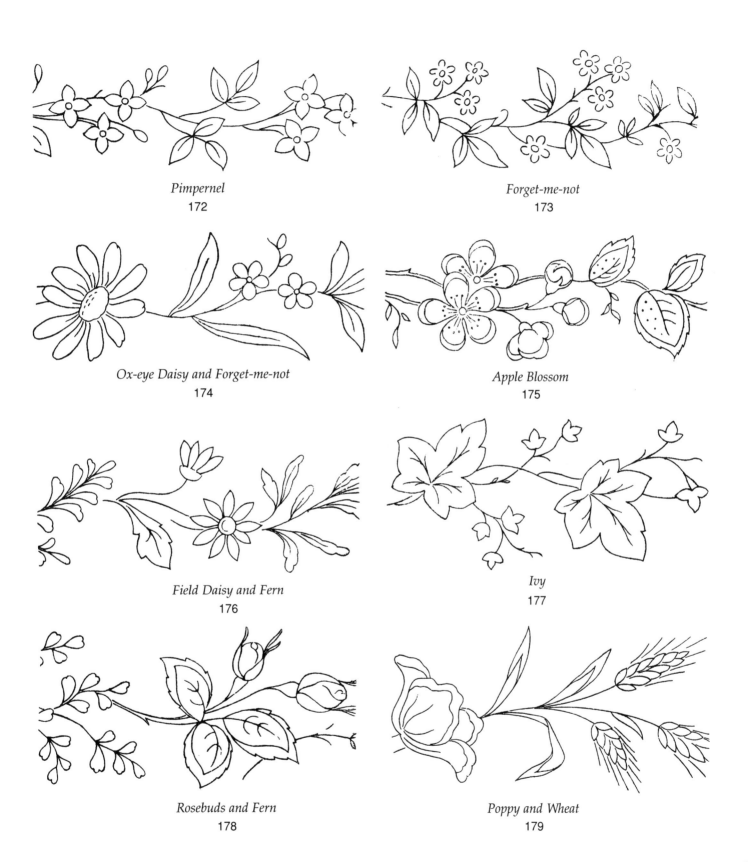

Pimpernel
172

Forget-me-not
173

Ox-eye Daisy and Forget-me-not
174

Apple Blossom
175

Field Daisy and Fern
176

Ivy
177

Rosebuds and Fern
178

Poppy and Wheat
179

Virginian Creeper
180

Wild Rose
181

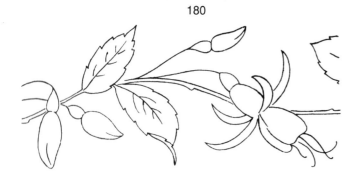

Fuchsia
182

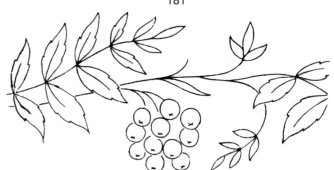

Mountain Ash
183

Jasmine
184

Jasmine and Rosebud
185

Wild Rose and Jasmine
186

Virginian Creeper
187